_____

Mom's Full

_____

Date of Birth

_____

Mom's Mother's Full Name

_____

Date of Birth   Place of Birth

_____

Mom's Father's Full Name

_____

Date of Birth   Place of Birth

My Mom

HER STORIES. HER WORDS.

COMPENDIUM.
live inspired

WITH SPECIAL THANKS TO THE ENTIRE COMPENDIUM FAMILY.

CREDITS:

Compiled by: Dan Zadra & Kristel Wills
Designed by: Steve Potter
Created by: Kobi Yamada

ISBN: 978-1-932319-63-7

Dear Mom...

In your hands you hold one of the most thoughtful gifts you could ever give your family. It won't take long for you to respond to the questions in this little book, but future generations will treasure your answers and your memories.

Imagine if your grandmother had been able to tuck away a similar book for you. What a joy to discover a few of her favorite memories of earlier days, in her own handwriting. Well, now is your chance to pick up a pen and create a wonderful family heirloom of your own.

Like a trip down memory lane, the following pages will whisk you back to another time and place. The questions are simple and straightforward, but only you can provide the answers—and that's what makes this book so special.

Mom, what music did you grow up listening to? What was your old neighborhood like? Who were your best friends? Have fun with your answers—they don't need to be complicated or formal. Just answer straight from the heart and the result is sure to be magical to those who love you.

Mom, what kind of house did you grow up in, and what was the old neighborhood like?

_____

_____

_____

_____

_____

_____

_____

_____

_____

_____

Mom, what was your favorite holiday as a child, and how did your family celebrate it?

_____

_____

_____

_____

_____

_____

_____

_____

_____

_____

Mom, what were some of the best presents you ever received
when you were a kid?

_____

_____

_____

_____

_____

_____

_____

_____

_____

Mom, who were your favorite pets, and what made them special?

_____

_____

_____

_____

_____

_____

_____

_____

_____

Mom, when you were a child, what did you want to be when you grew up? When you were a teenager? When you were a young adult?

_____

_____

_____

_____

_____

_____

_____

_____

_____

Mom, who were some of your favorite relatives, and what made them special?

_____

_____

_____

_____

_____

_____

_____

_____

_____

_____

Mom, what's your favorite memory of your mom? Your dad?

_____

_____

_____

_____

_____

_____

_____

_____

_____

Mom, what was your relationship like with your family when you were growing up?

_____

_____

_____

_____

_____

_____

_____

_____

_____

_____

Mom, what traits or characteristics do you have that your parents also had? And which side of your family do you most resemble?

_____

_____

_____

_____

_____

_____

_____

_____

_____

mom, what's the best thing your mom and/or dad taught you?

_____

_____

_____

_____

_____

_____

_____

_____

_____

Mom, what rules did your parents have, and which ones drove you crazy?

_____

_____

_____

_____

_____

_____

_____

_____

_____

_____

Mom, what are one or two things you did that you didn't tell your parents about?

_____

_____

_____

_____

_____

_____

_____

_____

_____

_____

Mom, what was the worst mischief you got into when you were younger?

_____

_____

_____

_____

_____

_____

_____

_____

_____

_____

Mom, what music did you grow up listening to?

_____

_____

_____

_____

_____

_____

_____

_____

_____

Mom, who were your best friends from childhood, and what were they like?

_____

_____

_____

_____

_____

_____

_____

_____

_____

_____

Mom, what are your favorite summer memories?

_____

_____

_____

_____

_____

_____

_____

_____

_____

_____

Mom, who was the best teacher you ever had, and why?

_____

_____

_____

_____

_____

_____

_____

_____

_____

_____

Mom, did you play a sport, and what did you like best about it?

_____

_____

_____

_____

_____

_____

_____

_____

_____

_____

mom, who taught you to drive, and what was your first car?

_____

_____

_____

_____

_____

_____

_____

_____

_____

_____

mom, what were your first few jobs? What did you do, and do you
remember how much you earned?

_____

_____

_____

_____

_____

_____

_____

_____

_____

_____

Mom, did you ever win an award you were proud of, and what was it in honor of?

_____

_____

_____

_____

_____

_____

_____

_____

_____

_____

Mom, how did you meet Dad, and what was your first date like?

_____

_____

_____

_____

_____

_____

_____

_____

_____

Mom, how did you spend your free time before you had kids?

_____

_____

_____

_____

_____

_____

_____

_____

_____

mom, what do you remember about the birth of your children?

_____

_____

_____

_____

_____

_____

_____

_____

_____

_____

Mom, what was it like for you to become a mother?

_____

_____

_____

_____

_____

_____

_____

_____

_____

mom, what's the best thing about being a mother?
What's the hardest thing?

_____

_____

_____

_____

_____

_____

_____

_____

_____

_____

mom, what are some favorite things you've done with your children?

_____

_____

_____

_____

_____

_____

_____

_____

_____

_____

mom, what advice would you pass along about being a mom?

_____

_____

_____

_____

_____

_____

_____

_____

_____

_____

Mom, looking back on your life, what are some of your proudest accomplishments?

_____

_____

_____

_____

_____

_____

_____

_____

_____

_____

mom, what are some ways—good or bad—the world has changed since you were a kid?

_____

_____

_____

_____

_____

_____

_____

_____

_____

Mom, where is the most interesting place you've ever visited,
and why?

_____

_____

_____

_____

_____

_____

_____

_____

_____

Mom, who are the people you most admire, and why?

_____

_____

_____

_____

_____

_____

_____

_____

_____

Mom, what are some of your favorite family recipes?

_____

_____

_____

_____

_____

_____

_____

_____

_____

_____

mom, what is the craziest or most impulsive thing you've ever done?

_____

_____

_____

_____

_____

_____

_____

_____

_____

_____

Mom, what is your perfect day?

_____

_____

_____

_____

_____

_____

_____

_____

_____

_____

Mom, if you could have three wishes, what would they be?

_____

_____

_____

_____

_____

_____

_____

_____

_____

mom, what are some things you still want to do in your lifetime?

_____

_____

_____

_____

_____

_____

_____

_____

_____

mom, how do you want future generations of your family to remember you?

_____

_____

_____

_____

_____

_____

_____

_____

_____

Of all the gifts she gave us, please,
the greatest of these were the memories.

—ISABELLA GRAHAM